COGNITIVE
BEHAVIORAL
THERAPY

*A Psychologist's Guide to Overcome Anxiety,
Depression & Negative Thought Patterns -
Simple Methods to Retrain Your Brain*

KATHERINE CHAMBERS

TABLE OF CONTENTS

INTRODUCTION

"What really frightens and dismays us is not external events themselves, but the way in which we think about them. It is not things that disturb us, but our interpretation of there significance"

(Epictetus)

If there is one thing I have learned from living life up until this point, it is this. As humans, we live out our days almost entirely within our own heads. That may seem like a trivial and obvious statement, but it couldn't be more true. It also has monumental implications on how a person will act in the world. But more importantly, the influence these thought patterns have over our emotional state.

How a person thinks and processes thoughts (especially if they are stressful and traumatic in nature) will have a huge impact on whether they are generally happy or sad. Whether they live in a constant state of fear, anxiety and frustration, or peace and harmony with the world.

It certainly isn't an easy thing to deal with, the processing of stressful situations and the negative implications they may bring. It plagues everyone of us to some degree, including me. So nobody should feel embarrassed about taking the right steps in dealing with it. It's your absolute base human right, to live a satisfying and fulfilling existence.

Cognitive behavioral therapy is really just a method to get people back on track. It is the intersection of a person's thoughts, behaviors and emotions. It's about combining certain therapeutic exercises from each part of this psychobehavioral matrix in order to rectify the unhinged and negative thought patterns within us. It's about taking elements of each, and combining them in a holistic manner to produce an overall positive effect on thinking and behavior.

In essence, CBT is about changing the ways the body and mind react to things.

My aim for this book is to give you an overview of the CBT principles which can help you do just that. To give you an understanding, as well as some pointers on how these basic (and some advanced) techniques are put into practice. To show you exactly what CBT style therapies can treat, and the benefits they can bring about.

However it is up to you to seek out a licensed professional to guide you through a proper CBT journey of sessions if you believe you require it. I am simply laying out the foundation for you here, to provide a better understanding of the principles.

I want to give you some initial guidance and provide some hope that your thinking can turn around for the better. There is certainly light at the end of the tunnel here. I have seen it happen within my own life, along with scores of other people in both clinical settings as well as everyday life. So approach these techniques with an open mind and you will surely gain a great deal from them.

My Credentials

Before we get into the ins and outs of Cognitive Behavioral Therapy, it's probably a good idea for me to explain exactly who I am, and why you should even bother listening to me in the first place. Yes I have the undergraduate and master's degree in psychology from Stanford, but my main focus over the past 15 years or so has been on the practical elements of the discipline. I wouldn't ever call myself a "Self-Help Guru" but I do focus much more on the results of these principles in the real world compared to my previous life of studying endless research papers on the academic side of the subject.

I use what I have learned and observe the behavior and psychological patterns of other successful people in life, to pin point exactly what it is they are doing to elicit the results they are achieving. There are common patterns to these people and behaviors if you know how to spot them. Fortunately for you even if you don't, I have spent the past 2 decades working this stuff out for you. I have dedicated my 40's to documenting both the rationale behind the most important psychological mindsets as well as the practical advice on how to cultivate the ability to use them to your benefit. In the real world.

It all started when I was just a young girl growing up on the east coast, I was a very observant kid. I was the youngest of four in our family which was fine with me as I would get to watch my older sister and brothers in action. Watch for their actions and behaviors, their successes and failures as almost a dry run for what I should be doing.

This continued through high school and into college, I luckily had a very active and ambitious peer group, it's hard not to when you live on the Stanford campus. I played a high level of lacrosse as well as track and field whilst at university so got to view the psychology of team/individual sports as well as in academia.

However it wasn't until I left college life and started living in the real world have I really developed a taste for the subjects I once studied. It's all well and good reading the intricacies of psychological theories from the comfort of your dorm room or library, but it's not until you have to put these theories to the test in life in general do you really understand how they work. It's not until you have to make your way in business, within a career, build a family for yourself do you really understand the impact your mindset has to your overall success.

For me that has been building a multi-six figure consulting business and now a family of my own. But I am not here to blow my own horn or preach in anyway, nobody needs that. What I will do is put things into perspective, what I know to be true from the science behind these principles, combined with my experience in the real world. I have made many mistakes along the way and will point out these pitfalls for you.

So why am I now writing about Cognitive Behavioral Therapy? As I mentioned, I studied a wide range of topics within the field of psychology and neuroscience whilst at college, which formed my base understanding of these principles. But I have since picked up many critical skill sets whilst building a family and career of my own. Everything from managing my personal and business relationships to my own mental state. Everything has been a learning curve and one which has taken deep emotional understanding and soul searching at times.

I am not an expert in CBT per se, however I have come to realize the great benefits it can provide a person through the application of it's various techniques. The real world is about problem solving, it's about rapport building with others and creating harmony within yourself most importantly.

However sometimes these things can go awry. They can start to frustrate you to the point of anger, distress and end in a spiral of unproductive thinking. As I mentioned in the open remarks to this book, this is not something to be ashamed of, it's a normal aspect of life. The key is in dealing with these tendencies and managing the thoughts, behaviors and emotions around these negative thought patterns.

So now that you know a little more about me, let's dive in. The following chapters will give you a sound overview of the main CBT strategies in order for you to better decide on your next course of action. This potentially might be therapy, if you so choose.

Similar to anger management exercises, a lot of this work involves identifying the underlying issues you have, and the triggers which set off negative thinking in the first place. So make sure you are as open and honest with yourself when going through these techniques. I promise you, it will be well worth it.

PART 1

A BASIC UNDERSTANDING
OF COGNITIVE BEHAVIORAL
THERAPY PRINCIPLES

Cognitive behavioral therapy is one of the most extensively used treatment modalities in the field of psychology today. Part 1 of this book will explain what CBT is, where it is used, and how it is done. Basic ideas and principles behind CBT will also be discussed.

CHAPTER 1

WHAT ACTUALLY IS CBT?

"There are a variety of techniques to help people change the kind of thinking that leads them to become depressed. These techniques are called cognitive behavioral therapy"

(Irving Kirsch)

A client walks into a psychologist's clinic. They are emotionally bothered and extremely overwhelmed with the myriad of problems they are currently facing. The person suffers from anxiety attacks, episodes of depression, and feelings of hopelessness. They were referred to a psychologist for CBT treatment.

But what exactly is Cognitive Behavioral Therapy? Where did it originate, and how is it primarily done? And is this therapy a working treatment which can help eliminate certain mental health disturbances?

Cognitive Behavioral Therapy Defined

Cognitive Behavioral Therapy (CBT) is a combined psychotherapy and behavioral therapy treatment aimed at changing the way a person thinks and acts towards stressful situations they may be buried in. It is a treatment used by many psychologists to help their clients beat several mental health problems. CBT employs a practical approach to help the client identify their problems and help them think and act more positively towards them.

The main goal of cognitive behavioral therapy is to alter a person's mindset and actions to drive them towards acceptable actions about their problems. CBT can be thought of as a scientific approach to problem-solving for clients who are heavily burdened and do not know what to do with their life problems.

Depression is the main mental health disturbance that cognitive behavioral therapy addresses. It was also depression which led to the discovery of CBT in the first place. However, the therapy has been proven effective in treating many other cases of mental health problems since then.

Health Problems Treated by Cognitive Behavioral Therapy

Apart from clinical depression, the following mental health problems respond positively to cognitive behavioral therapy:

- Phobias

- Post-Traumatic Stress Disorder (PTSD)

- Obsessive-Compulsive Disorder (OCD)

- Anorexia and Bulimia Nervosa – Eating Disorders

- Anxiety Attacks

- Insomnia and Sleep Disturbances

- Alcoholism

- Relationship problems

- Repetitive habits that are disturbing

- Mood swings

- Anger Management

CBT is not exclusively used for treating mental disturbances alone. The therapy has also been proven effective in helping clients with long-term illnesses cope with the demands and hardships of their sickness. Long-term illnesses make these patients feel hopeless, causing their coping mechanisms to fail, paving the way for depression to sink in.

CBT is especially useful for clients inflicted with the following long-term and/or lifelong illnesses, including but not limited to:

- Chronic Fatigue Syndrome

- Diabetes Mellitus

- Hypertension

- Irritable Bowel Syndrome

- Kidney Problems/Kidney Failure

History of Cognitive Behavioral Therapy

Dr. Aaron T. Beck discovered the concepts behind cognitive behavioral therapy during his work as a psychiatrist at the University of Pennsylvania in the 1960's. Dr. Beck was carrying out research on psychoanalysis and depression. He went on to test and validate his concepts by applying them to various experiments involving his clients, who mostly consisted of depressed people. But what he discovered was not really what he had expected. He had uncovered the Automatic Thoughts concept, and how it is closely related to depression episodes.

The Automatic Thoughts Concept

In automatic thoughts, the depressed person experiences negative thoughts continuously, as if someone has pushed an automatic button and flooded their mind with negativity all the time. Automatic thoughts reside in a person's negative perception of the events surrounding his or her life.

Dr. Beck grouped automatic thoughts into three categories:

1. **Negative self-image** – The depressed person has continuous negative thoughts and ideas about themselves as a person. They forget to realize their worth as an individual, and thus

continuously belittles themselves, leading to a negative self-image which is very difficult to change.

2. **Negative world around them** – The depressed person perceives the world negatively, thinking only about the bad things that happen around their life. They only see the sadness, pain, and hurt that their present life is giving them. They are unable to see the beauty which lies in the events happening around them.

3. **Negative future** – The depressed person also views their future in a negative manner. They lose all hope for a better life as they continuously negate the present moment and thinks that the future will hold no good to them. They automatically discount any possible improvement in their situation going forward.

As a result of automatic thoughts, Dr. Beck uncovered the reasons why depressed people stay in their miserable states for a very long time. And with that, he looked for clinical ways to help his clients combat the negativity which leads to long-term depression.

How Negative Automatic Thoughts Are Developed

Dr. Beck concluded that negative thoughts residing in the adult mind are formed way back, as early as a person's childhood days.

Dysfunctional assumption is a term he used to describe a certain rule which allows a person to thrive on a certain behavior based on a past experience.

An example of this may go something like this. A child who is constantly being bullied at school learns that when he goes along with what his friends love to do, he doesn't get bullied at all. He then forms this dysfunctional assumption "I have to follow what my friends love doing so that they will stop giving me a hard time."

However, if some kind of event gives him a failure to follow his dysfunctional assumptions, negative automatic thoughts start creeping in. In the above example, the child might start to think, "They're bullying me again. I wasn't able to do stuff that they like. I really can't please anybody. They don't like me, and I'm a total mess."

These thoughts ultimately affect the person's behavior. The child in the example might suddenly withdraw from his friends, keep himself preoccupied with small things, refuse to meet other children, and become aloof in his own little world. If not prevented, negative automatic thoughts will be carried over to adulthood, where the vicious cycle of negativity continues as the person experiences more problems along the way.

Fighting Automatic Thoughts and the Dawn of Cognitive Behavioral Therapy

Dr. Beck started to help his clients admit, identify, validate, and evaluate their automatic thoughts. His clients minds were awoken after having them evaluate their negative impressions about themselves and about their lives. They were able to sync with their positive selves emotionally, giving them better feelings and a new hope to rise from the negativity which has engulfed them.

Dr. Beck's clients then began to change their mindsets and improve their perception of themselves, the world, and their future lives. Since they already felt better about themselves, they were able to focus more on improving their behaviors. This lead them to becoming more functional individuals again, slowly erasing traces of the depression which they had held for so long.

With all these, Dr. Beck discovered that changing the way a person thinks about themselves and others, is key to helping them rise from depressed thoughts and enter a realm of long-lasting behavioral and cognitive change. He termed his new clinical approach to depression as "Cognitive Therapy", to be known later on as "Cognitive Behavioral Therapy".

Characteristics of Cognitive Behavioral Therapy

While modern-day cognitive behavioral therapies may slightly differ in practice, they all share these common characteristics:

CBT is based on facts and evidence-based research. Several studies have been undertaken regarding CBT, its effectiveness, and how it must be utilized to help mental health clients recover and return to their normal lives.

CBT is a short-term therapy. The duration usually takes five to twenty sessions, with the client attending 30-60 minute sessions either once a week or twice a month every two weeks.

CBT is an organized therapy program. All qualified CBT therapists and practitioners follow a standard method to keep their clients focused on changing their behaviors for the better.

It's not the event which causes the depression, it's the thinking behind this particular event which triggers a flood of negative emotions within a person. They give meanings to these life events and believe they are the culprit of their depression, making the person upset, irritable, and saddened all the time.

Changing a client's negative mindset and perceptions is key to improving their behavioral patterns and emotions. The client is allowed to look at a certain stimulus and react to it until they gradually change their perception of it. They will then in turn start to positively change the way in which they will behave toward that same unchanged stimulus.

What Happens in a CBT Session?

Other psychological therapies commonly ask the client to freely talk about what's on their mind. But in CBT, a structured treatment plan is followed, making it different from other treatments.

Basically, the client and therapist work together to achieve the goals they've jointly set. Collaborative empiricism, a term Dr. Beck used to describe the collaborative work between the therapist and client, is a main feature of cognitive behavioral therapy.

The therapy session starts when the therapist meets the client and starts building rapport with them. After this, the client is asked to verbalize their specific problems. It could be uncomfortable symptoms troubling them, or life problems that keep them agitated and stressed-out.

Upon assessing the client's targeted problems, the therapist helps the client form goals that will become the foundation of every CBT session from then on. They both determine what goals to set, what topics to focus on each week, and how to meet each targeted goal within the specific time frames they've set.

During each CBT session, the therapist gives their client homework assignments – activities which allow the client to express their thoughts and feelings. These assignments also help the therapist assess, plan, and shape their client's new mindset. Examples of homework may include keeping a diary of the client's depressive thoughts, learning coping mechanisms in order to shut out anxiety, or meeting a friend at some place as part of learning how to cope with social anxiety.

The therapist gives the client enough time to review what they've learned from the previous session. They will also let the client know about the progress they've made on previously completed homework assignments.

In summary, the structured one-to-one CBT therapy lets the therapist guide the client in finding ways to solve their problems. They set a goal, the therapist gives the client assignments, they talk about these assignments and practice what they've learned from them. Then, they evaluate the principles and insights acquired from these activities, and let the client integrate these insights into reaching their problem-solving goals.

CHAPTER 2

UNDERSTANDING ANXIETY & DEPRESSION

"Cognitive therapy seeks to alleviate psychological stresses by correcting faulty conceptions and self-signals. By correcting erroneous beliefs, we can lower excessive reactions"

(Aaron Beck)

Two of the most common mental disturbances CBT can help to eliminate are anxiety and depression. Many people who are feeling a little down in the dumps may claim that they have either one of these conditions, or possibly both. But what does anxiety and depression really mean? And when is CBT needed to combat these two mental disturbances?

Definition of Anxiety

Anxiety is defined as the body's normal reaction to upcoming stressful events. It's the feeling of distress and uneasiness a person typically experiences prior to a big event in his or her life, which is on the horizon. For example, that jittery sensation a person feels before performing in front of a crowd, or the unrest someone automatically feels before taking an important exam. This is actually healthy anxiety.

In its core essence, anxiety is not a mental disturbance. It is actually a healthy and normal reaction the body produces in response to anticipating a stressful event. It's a natural feeling which simply goes away once a person is already someway into the stressful experience. Anxiety actually aids a person in staying focused and alert, providing a positive overall effect on performance.

When Anxiety Becomes Abnormal

Not everyone is fortunate enough to experience just this normal form of anxiety. Some people suffer from Anxiety Disorder. A legitimate condition which requires careful consideration by a health care professional. It's a type of mental disturbance wherein a person suffers from irrational anxiety, which has gone overboard. Its usually expressed as an excessive and inappropriate response to a current situation, or anticipated future event.

People with anxiety disorder have episodes which suddenly creep into their thinking. It consumes them, often in normal, everyday situations. Anxiety disorder can also recur often, and sufferers feel as if they have completely lost all control when these anxious impulses do arise.

Types of Anxiety Disorders

Anxiety disorder isn't a single type of mental disturbance. There are in fact a number of ways in which it can come to light. The following are conditions which can be classified as anxiety disorders:

1. **Panic Attacks** – A person inflicted with this disorder experiences sudden bouts of repetitive feelings of terror and panic. Panic attacks can come without warning and cause a person to feel like they are having a heart attack in extreme cases.

2. **Social Anxiety Disorder** – This disorder causes a person to feel overwhelmingly conscious in normal day-to-day social interactions. It stems from a strong fear of being judged and a fear of being publicly humiliated. People with social anxiety disorder may dread social functions and activities which forces them to go out and interact with others. It can also keep them from creating friendships, establishing romantic relationships, and interacting with the general public.

3. **Separation Anxiety** – This type of anxiety disorder occurs when a person gets that overwhelming fear of being left alone by someone important to them. They fear being alone and crave the presence of a particular person, making it irrationally hard for them to separate from that person. This type of anxiety often occurs most frequently in toddlers and children, but can persist into adulthood.

4. **Phobias** – This anxiety disorder stems from a strong and inappropriate fear of a certain object or activity. This strong fear disables a person from operating in everyday situations related to the thing they fear most. Phobias are varied, and can range from fear of heights or flying to the fear of insects. People experiencing phobias may perform avoidance activities just to keep them away from the thing or activity they are so afraid of.

5. **Generalized Anxiety Disorder** – This type of anxiety disorder is characterized by a strong and constant sense of fear and worry. These feelings have no direct trigger and may come to the person in a flash. Anxiety also comes often, making the person unable to go on with their daily activities. The trigger-free anxiety people with Generalized Anxiety Disorder feel is termed Free-Floating Anxiety.

The root cause of the above mentioned mental disturbances is unexplained anxiety. This inexplicable anxiety may or may not have a triggering factor.

But aside from those mental disturbances, anxiety disorder may also be present in people suffering from other mental health conditions where the anxiety isn't the main focus of the problem. These conditions include:

- Eating Disorders

- Personality Disorders

- Clinical Depression

Symptoms of Anxiety Disorder

The specific symptoms of anxiety disorder may vary depending on the person's particular disturbance. But there are common symptoms which most sufferers share. They include the following:

- Sudden and uncontrollable feelings of panic and worry

- Sweaty and cold hands and feet

- Inability to stay calm

- Restlessness

- Muscle tension

- Heart palpitations

- Inability to concentrate

- Dry mouth

- Shortness of breath

- Nausea

- Dizziness

- Tingling and numbness of the hands and feet

Causes of Anxiety Disorders

Anxiety disorders may stem from various causes, depending on the person and their individual circumstances. The causes could be a mixture of several physical and chemical factors happening within the person's body. Contrary to popular belief, anxiety disorders are not predominantly caused by improper upbringing or character weakness. Rather, the following factors are more influential in causing the disorder:

- Dysfunction within the regions of the brain related to fear and stress regulation

- Changes in the brains memory regulating centers

- Chemical imbalances

- Genetic or hereditary factors; inherited from either side of a family

- Long-standing stress

- Traumatic events or memories

- Substance and/or alcohol abuse

- Medication side-effects

- Other related mental health issues that may cause a flare-up of anxiety

Treating Anxiety with CBT

Cognitive behavioral therapy is one of the chosen treatment modalities used in clients with various kinds of anxiety disorders. It's one of the most widely used therapeutic treatments for anxiety.

People with anxiety disorders must have their negative thoughts slowly altered and replaced with positive ones. This enables them to perceive and associate more positive emotions with regards to the things they're anxious of. By changing the way a person thinks about their fears and anxieties, they can simultaneously change the way they feel and behave towards that situation.

CBT uses Cognitive Restructuring in order to change the person's negative thoughts. Cognitive restructuring is also known as "thought challenging". Here, the therapist identifies a client's negative thoughts and challenges them through three steps:

1. Identifying the person's negative thoughts.

2. Challenging these negative thoughts through evaluation, then finding evidence to disprove the negative thoughts.

3. Introducing more rational and realistic thoughts to replace the negative ones.

Therapists may also teach their clients the following techniques during their CBT sessions:

- Ways to recognize the feelings of anxiety.

- Facing the client's fears in a rational way.

- Coping techniques to help the client relax and counteract panicky and anxious feelings in a positive manner.

Definition of Depression

First, it's important to state that it is normal to feel sad and down at times. Sadness is a normal human emotion which people feel as a result of momentary life struggles and/or the loss of something or someone. It's an inescapable facet of life.

But clinical depression is different. This prevalent mental disturbance goes far beyond the typical sadness which everyone feels from time to time.

Clinical depression, also known as major depressive disorder, is defined as an overwhelming feeling of intense sadness that can last for weeks or even months at a time, and acutely hinders a person's daily activities in every sense.

Diagnosing Clinical Depression

The key hallmarks of true depression are continuing depressed moods and a notable diminishing of any interest in activities which a person previously enjoyed doing. Either of these symptoms must be present in a person on a daily basis, or almost daily for two weeks in order for it to be confirmed as clinical depression.

In addition to this, depression can also be diagnosed using the guidelines in the DSM-5 Manual. If a person experiences at least five of the following eight symptoms, for a minimum of two weeks, then they can be considered clinically depressed:

1. Depressed mood throughout the entire day, but most markedly during mornings.

2. A huge loss of interest in previously enjoyed activities.

3. Repetitive suicidal thoughts or having great desire to die.

4. Intense feelings of guilt and worthlessness everyday.

5. Unrelenting restlessness.

6. Inability to concentrate and make decisions.

7. Sudden surge of weight loss or weight gain.

8. Frequent insomnia or hypersomnia which occurs daily or almost daily.

A person exhibiting these symptoms will often appear physically distressed and/or impaired. This is another contributing factor in the overall diagnosis of clinical depression.

Note that these symptoms must stand on their own and must not be caused by a side effect of any other medication, in order to truly pass as clinical depression. They must also not be a direct result of a pre-existing medical condition.

Factors Related to the Development of Depression

It's also important to note, that nobody can be completely inoculated from feeling this way. It can happen to anybody, regardless of his or her socio-economic status. Even if a person lives in perceived total comfort and has all of the monetary and material wealth in the world, they are still not immune from developing depression.

Although there are certain instances, mainly traumatic in nature which can be seen to set off episodes of depression, such as returning military personnel from war torn regions or car accident patients. There doesn't seem to be any definite casual links that predetermine a likelihood of depression within "normal" everyday life. External factors may play a role in developing depression, but other factors come into play which include the following:

1) **Chemical Composition of the Brain** – Depressed people usually exhibit imbalances in brain chemical compositions. This can greatly contribute to the various depressive symptoms a person feels.

2) **Life Outlook and Personality** – Some people can exhibit a pessimistic life outlook even without depression. But if this negative perspective persists, it might well develop into full-

blown depression at some point in the persons life. People who easily get agitated by stress, and those who have low self-esteem are also somewhat more vulnerable to developing depression.

3) **Environmental Factors** – Similar to the traumatic instances I described previously, poverty, abuse, violence, and neglect may also contribute to the development of depression in a person. These negative experiences often push a person to their limits which predisposes them to depressive tendencies.

4) **Heredity and Genetics** – Depression can be passed on from generations of families. A parent who had depression may pass this on to their children. A similar observation can be view within twins I.e. if one twin is exhibiting depressive symptoms, there is a 50-70% chance the other will also develop such tendencies. Although the specific casual links within the individuals DNA makeup have not yet been pinpointed.

5) **Medical Conditions** – Lifelong medical illnesses such as diabetes and incurable cancers may also serve as a trigger for developing depression.

Symptoms of Clinical Depression

While the symptoms previously mentioned from the DSM-5 Manual help guide clinicians in determining the diagnosis of clinical depression, there are other common symptoms which most depressed people generally experience and serve as a good guide for anybody worried about their current mental well-being. They are as follows:

- Persistent sadness and feelings of emptiness.

- A pessimistic outlook on life.

- Loss of interest in daily activities.

- Loss of interest in life as a whole.

- Irritability.

- Frequent sleeping or inability to sleep.

- Decreased energy and fatigue.

- Bodily aches, cramps, headaches, and digestive tract problems that do not alleviate even when treated.

- Overeating and/or loss of appetite.

Not all depressed people experience all of these symptoms at once. It depends entirely on the severity of the condition within each individual case.

Types of Depression

Depression doesn't just manifest itself as one well-defined illness either. It comes in many different forms, as varied as the reasons for its existence. These include the following:

- **Major Depressive Disorder** – This is the main type of clinical depression which is diagnosed today, where a person experiences a persistent depressive or negative mood for at least two weeks.

- **Chronic Depression** – This disorder is also called dysthymia or mild depression. Symptoms are usually milder than major depression, but they last longer, usually around two years or more. People with dysthymia may also experience bouts of major depression, and this is termed Double Depression.

- **Seasonal Affective Disorder** – This depressive state often occurs in relation to seasonal changes. Most people manifest moodiness and sadness starting during the fall season and continues well into winter. Affected persons often feel better during spring and summer months when there is an increased amount of ultraviolet sunlight producing higher levels of vitamin D within them.

- **Postpartum Depression** – Mothers who have recently given birth often experience the baby blues – an overwhelming period wherein they experience moodiness, crying spells, and anxiety for a few days and up to two weeks after giving birth. This may continue to become postpartum depression, a saddened state where mothers often experience more intense symptoms which interfere with their abilities to care for their newborns.

- **Bipolar Depression** – Also known as manic depression, bipolar depression is a disorder characterized by extremes of emotions. The bipolar person may feel extreme mania or intense happiness on some days, then dip down into severe depression on the other end.

- **Psychotic Depression** – This is a severe form of clinical depression wherein the person experiences complex symptoms such as delusions, paranoia, or hallucinations. Suicidal thoughts often linger in people afflicted with this disorder, making it a psychiatric emergency due to a high risk for suicide and death.

- **Substance-Induced Mood Disorder** – Abuse of alcohol, opioids, and other similar substances may trigger the depressive symptoms found in substance-induced mood disorder.

Treating Depression with CBT

Cognitive behavioral therapy is certainly a popular treatment with regards to helping clients suffering from any of the various types of clinical depression discussed here. The chances of recovering from depression are high in clients who have undergone professional and thorough CBT sessions.

As explained in the previous chapter, CBT generally describes how a person's behavior and moods are defined by his or her thought patterns. Hence, CBT helps reshape a client's behavior by helping them identify their own negative thought patterns, check if these thoughts are really appropriate, and come up with healthier pathways to replace all of the negativity in their mind.

Using CBT to overcome depression works in a similar way with anxiety treatments. Therapists also use cognitive restructuring to mold and shape the client's thought patterns into more positive ones. More on this later.

Once the client learns to replace his or her negative thoughts with more realistic ones, their mood should gradually improve. Their behaviors then follow the same positive pattern their mind has now created. The person should begin to rekindle their interest in life and in the various activities they once previously shunned. Most importantly, they will be able to return to activities of daily living with minimal struggles and with a more optimistic outlook on the future.

CBT therapy in mild to moderately depressed clients can be as effective as antidepressants in many cases. However for clients with major depression, CBT combined with pharmaceutical drug use is usually the preferred plan of action. At least to begin with. This form of treatment should always be tapered-off in favor of more holistic and natural methods as soon as considered safe to do so.

CHAPTER 3

IDENTIFYING THOUGHT PATTERNS - BREAKING NEGATIVE ONES

"The greatest weapon against stress is our ability to choose one thought over another"

(William James)

Cognitive behavioral therapy implies that negative thought patterns must be slowly eradicated from a client's mind, and must be replaced with more realistic thought patterns. Or certainly more beneficial ones. As a therapist, how would one learn to recognize and identify these negative thought patterns?

What Is Negative Thinking?

Negative thinking is simply defined as a thought process which brings about negative consequences. A person consumed with negative thoughts predominantly focuses on the worst possible outcomes in almost every situation they face. They often see the worst side of everything, always taking into account things which may go wrong in every move they make.

Types of Negative Thoughts

Therapists must assist their clients in identifying their negative thoughts first an foremost. Here are some common types of negative thinking patterns which a therapist may usually encounter:

- **Labelling Oneself Negatively** – This type of thinking leads a person to believe they are naturally filled with flaws, and subsequently they're already failures in life.

- **Catastrophizing** – People who always think of the worst-case scenario in any situation they find themselves in and are always fearful of the outcome. Catastrophizing an event is a common thought type for this subset of people. Sound familiar?

- **Magical Thoughts** – This thought pattern is often seen in children and in those afflicted with obsessive-compulsive disorder and bipolar disorders. People who regularly indulge in magical thoughts often believe in certain rituals that they must perform to save themselves or others from harm. Or at least alleviate some form of dissonance and discomfort in their mind.

- **Perfectionist Thinking** – People who consistently indulge this type of thinking believe they must do everything perfectly in order to gain the approval of others. Anything less than perfect in their actions is an automatic failure on their part. Similar to an obsessive-compulsive type of thinking, these individuals find it hard to move on as they are continuously revising the task at hand, ensuring overall progress in life is slow.

- **Mind Reading** – This thought pattern occurs when a person assumes they know exactly what others are thinking and that they do not approve of their behaviors. They believe they can read other people's minds which gives them a false and negative impression of themselves which can seriously hit their ego and self-esteem.

- **Approval-Seeking** – This person seeks continuous approval from the people around them. If someone isn't happy about something, they innately assume it's somehow a result of their actions, and seek to rectify the situation immediately.

- **Pessimistic Life Outlook** – Viewing life as nothing but a continuous struggle qualifies a person under the pessimistic negative thought pattern process. This is a very common predisposition in society, as it's the perfect safety mechanism for when things inevitably go wrong. People will fall back on statements like "I told you this wouldn't work out for us".

- **Paranoia** – This thought pattern occurs when a person believes that everyone he or she meets are watching them and judging their actions. It's a thinking habit which is a very close cousin to the 'Mind Reading' principle stated above. They go hand in hand and often perpetuate one another.

- **Serious Delusional Thinking** – Each of the aforementioned negative thought types have some form of mild delusions to them. But serious delusional thinking often involves strange beliefs with no solid basis to reality whatsoever. This thought process is usually seen in severe forms of paranoia or depression.

The negative thought processes mentioned here may sometimes be tricky to recognize in a client. They might exhibit one or more of these thinking patterns combined together. Negative thinkers also usually keep their thought patterns under wraps, making them hard to uncover. This is why the therapist must be skilled at successfully identifying and carefully discerning each negative thought pattern during the course of CBT sessions.

Where Negative Thinking Leads

It goes without saying that people who think negatively all of the time, tend to lead unhappy and fearful lives. Each time they think of a negative thought, they bring about negative consequences in their lives. Ultimately, their behaviors become so pessimistic that it gets out of control and leads them to actions and decisions which are only based on their fears, worries, and anxieties. It's like a perpetuating self-fulfilling prophecy of negativity.

Take for instance a woman who wants to consider taking home a pet cat. She is open to the idea of having a cat for companionship, but is suddenly overwhelmed by the negative thoughts repeatedly entering her mind. She may state something like this:

"I'd love to bring home a pet cat, but cats are often messy and are hard to play with. They do nothing but break fragile vases, chase after mice, and get themselves tangled in lots of household messes. I cannot afford to have a cat for a pet, what with all of these potential problems I'd have to worry about."

In the example above, the woman was focusing entirely on the disadvantages a pet cat would bring to her. She fears that a cat cannot live up to her standards of being a good pet companion. These disadvantages are her negative automatic thoughts. The negative thought pattern she has towards pet cats leads her to deter the idea of keeping one at home.

Hence, negative thinking eventually leads to negative decisions which bring about unpleasant consequences to the person involved. The negative thinker often experiences worry, fear, sadness and stress before an event which ultimately ensures they garner a negative result. Or certainly forego the positive benefits they would have received by just giving it a go. But again, it's all about perception here.

How Do Negative Thoughts Get Reinforced?

When a person believes in something, they are bound to get attracted to that particular thought. To seek out evidence for their reasoning. And when they repeatedly believe those specific thoughts are "true", it eventually becomes their reality.

This is a normal tendency in life. Humans are essentially pattern seekers by nature. We like to connect the dots in our thinking with regards to our environment. It's an ingrained evolutionary trait which has ensured our species has gotten to where we are today. "If it's true for you, then it is true" is a very accurate statement.

However these mental shortcuts aren't always beneficial, to say they do not serve the person well. This is what happens with regards to negative thought patterns. They get reinforced simply because the person holds on to them, believing them to be true.

Take for instance this example. A person thinking "I can never achieve my dreams" chooses to believe that he or she doesn't have the capacity to work towards fulfilling their dreams. Every time this thought pattern comes to their mind, the more they believe it to be accurate. And while they continuously believe they'll never get what they want out of life, the more it becomes ingrained into their subconscious mind. As a result, the essence of their negative beliefs slowly become a reality for them.

How to Identify Negative Thought Patterns

People suffering from continuous negative thoughts often fall into a saddened state of depression. That's why it is important to cut out these negative thoughts at the earliest possible time in order to avoid further pessimism, and to raise the person to a more optimistic and capable state.

In CBT, the first step in helping a client overcome their mental disturbances is identifying the client's negative thought patterns. It's quite hard to decipher negative thought patterns because these rhythms often become so ingrained within a person's subconscious mind.

The therapist's goal is to assist the client in identifying and viewing these negative thoughts for what they are. Helping the client become aware of these thoughts is the first step in dissolving negativity and ultimately aids in replacing them with more realistic and beneficial ones.

Here are some of the ways a therapist can identify negative thought patterns within a client:

Establish Good Rapport.

Upon meeting the client for the first time, the therapist must approach him or her in a kind, respectful, and non-judgmental manner. This will help establish rapport, a much-needed starting point for a healthy relationship with the client.

The therapist should also start picking up verbal cues from the client as they are freely talking about their thoughts. He or she must carefully observe and assess the way in which their client is inferring things. For instance, if the client talks hurriedly about their fears, or that someone is watching and judging their moves, then the therapist may already imply they have paranoid thoughts. Or, if the client talks in a bragging manner, they could have a negative perfectionist thinking mentality already presenting itself.

Pick-Up Nonverbal Cues.

Alongside the actual words and phrases a person is likely to use within a therapy session, clients often display nonverbal cues while interacting which can equally give away the mindset they find themselves in. It's up to the therapist to observe these nonverbal cues, such as tone of voice, gestures, facial expressions, posture, and gaze. These cues reveal more of what a person really thinks, in addition to the words they've been speaking to the therapist.

Breaking Negativity

Once the client is already aware of the negative thoughts consuming them, the therapist now starts to act in breaking the negativity surrounding the client's mind. This is where cognitive behavioral therapy sets in. Breaking negativity through CBT involves the following steps:

Analyzing the Client's Identified Thoughts

The therapist and client work together to analyze the underlying causes behind the client's identified negative thoughts. Questions to ask while studying the persons thoughts include:

- What circumstances have made the client think of such thoughts?

- What problems are responsible for making these thoughts ingrained within the person?

- Are these thoughts really helpful in solving the client's underlying problems?

Once the underlying issues which underpin these negative thoughts have been clearly identified, the therapist and client now shift to the next step.

Breaking Down Problems into Smaller Parts

By now, the client has grasped the fact that his or her negative thoughts do not contribute at all in solving their life problems. So together along with the therapist, they break down the persons problems into smaller chunks to slowly come up with ample solutions to them.

The therapist gives homework for the client to accomplish depending on the problems they have. Homework such as keeping a diary of their thoughts or meeting up with a long-time friend will help them shift their focus from negative thoughts, to more realistic and positive ones. This will help them find solutions to their problems in a more realistic and natural manner.

Acknowledging What Needs to Be Changed

The above process should give the client some reflection time where they should come to realize that they need to change something within themselves (if the initial sessions where carried out clearly and effectively). As they carry out these tasks prior to the next CBT session, they should slowly become more aware of the need to shun out negativity in order to accomplish things in a positive and beneficial way.

Breaking Free from Pessimistic Thoughts

As the CBT sessions continue, the client and therapist both realize what needs to be changed in the client's mindset. They jointly evaluate goals, discuss conclusions from previous sessions, and keep track of the client's progress in replacing their pessimistic thoughts.

The client then slowly learns how to shift his or her thinking to a more positive outlook. They finally accept that negative thoughts do nothing but deter them from solving their problems and living life fully and harmoniously. They will then start to naturally adopt a positive demeanor and apply this to creating solutions for the perceived problems at hand.

As a result, the client enters a pessimistic-free thought pattern cycle which eventually relieves him or her from the depressive symptoms they have been experiencing. They are able to resume their normal daily activities with the aid of this renewed positive outlook on life. One that should perpetuate indefinitely if the CBT sessions were effective in guiding the person to these conclusions. Other people will take a little more guidance if they start to slip back into the older, unproductive thought patterns.

As with all of the techniques within this book, breaking seriously damaging negative thought patterns should be done in conjunction with a proper professional. However in my personal experience, some simple NLP exercises can help here. I write about these strategies in greater detail within *"NLP: A Psychologist's Guide"*. However, I have included a chapter from that book at the end of this one, as it details a technique in identifying and breaking negative thought patterns with interrupts. So make sure you give it a try.

CHAPTER 4

ADDRESSING MALADAPTIVE
COPING MECHANISMS

People naturally use coping mechanisms to react to the various events happening in their lives. But people living with mental disturbances tend to use maladaptive ways in coping with their struggles. As a CBT therapist, how can one recognize and address these maladaptive coping mechanisms?

Coping Mechanisms Explained

People will naturally experience different stressful and anxiety-provoking situations in their daily lives, be it positive events such as the birth of a baby, or negative ones such as a job loss. This is why we require strategies to deal with these situations, to manage the emotions which arise, and keep them in check. These strategies are called Coping Mechanisms.

Coping mechanisms are combinations of thoughts, emotions, and outward behavior geared towards helping a person adjust to the amount of stress they are dealing with. Coping mechanisms keep people's emotions intact and prevent them from breaking out into full scale panic attacks due to large amounts of stress.

Coping Mechanisms versus Defense Mechanisms

Many people get confused with these two terms, believing they are one in the same thing. In fact, although these two mechanisms do share some similarities, they're never entirely the same.

Coping mechanisms are strategies which are consciously used by a person to lessen the impact of stress in their daily activities. A person can freely and consciously decide what strategies they would like to use in order to combat stress. Coping strategies consciously modify emotional and cognitive appraisals, leading to a visible change of reactions in relation to the stressful events happening to a person.

Defense mechanisms, on the other hand, are more accurately defined as unconscious processes which arise when a person is confronted with anxiety-provoking situations. These actions and thought patterns happen without the person's conscious intentions or choice. Defense mechanisms often distort a person's perception of events, leading them to think their realities have changed for the better.

Coping mechanisms and defense mechanisms can simultaneously activate in times of stress and anxiety. They both aid in stopping the build-up of negative emotions, only they do so in slightly different ways.

Types of Coping Mechanisms

There are several coping strategies which psychologists and researchers have been studying extensively. It would be impossible to list down all 400 to 600 coping mechanisms under research today. Hence, coping mechanisms are broadly classified into three main category types which are as follows:

1. **Emotion-Focused** – These are the coping strategies geared towards modifying one's emotions to compensate the stress being experienced. Meditation and relaxation techniques are examples of such strategies.

2. **Appraisal-Focused** – These coping mechanisms modify a person's thoughts and mindset in order to tolerate the stress. Denial is an example of this mechanism type.

3. **Problem-Focused** – Problem-solving skills are employed to change a person's behavior towards a particular stressful situation. The person first identifies the stress-inducing problem, then comes up with possible solutions to manage it.

Apart from these three strategies, there are several other common coping mechanisms which people often utilize, such as:

- **Humor and Fun** – Perceiving stress in a humorous way enables a person to laugh in the midst of stressful events and make light of such situations. This can highly reduce the negative impact on the person.

- **External Support Systems** – Having someone to talk to, such as a trusted friend or a counselor, significantly lessens stress levels and keeps a person's emotions intact.

- **Physical Activities** – Some people pour their energy into physical activities such as yoga, running, swimming, walking and cycling. This helps channel their unpleasant and stressful thoughts into more productive and healthy stress-relieving activities.

What Are Maladaptive Coping Mechanisms?

Most of the time, people are able to choose adaptive or positive coping mechanisms to resolve problems and reduce stress and anxiety. But there will be times in which a person uses maladaptive coping mechanisms.

Maladaptive coping mechanisms, also known as non-coping, are conscious strategies used only to reduce the symptoms of stress and anxiety. These strategies do not tend to lead to a total resolution of the problem at large.

A person using maladaptive coping mechanisms is unable to learn how to be totally free from the problems which have caused him or her worry, stress, and anxiety. These coping strategies just momentarily detach the person away from their fears, but the problem underlying the anxiety's root cause remains.

Types of Maladaptive Coping Mechanisms

These are the five most common maladaptive coping strategies used by people who suffer from persistent negative thought processes:

- **Avoidance** – This is where a person tends to avoid situations which cause them stress and worry. The avoidant person never gets a chance to face and overcome his or her problems, fears, anxieties. At least not whilst they are avoiding dealing with them honestly.

- **Aggression** – Here, a person may use anger to suppress his or her fears, doubts, and worries. Hostility and anger act as a large lid which shuts out painful emotional feelings. But using anger to cope with stress only leads to a cycle of more anger in the long run, harming not only the person harboring it, but also those around them. I write much more extensively on this and the strategies required to break these cycles within *"Anger Management: A Psychologist's Guide"*.

- **Short-term Focus/Relief** – This is a type of maladaptive strategy wherein a person quickly finds a way to relieve themselves of emotional pain right at the very start. They focus on building a wall to separate their thoughts and feelings from themselves. While this provides quick relief from stress and pain, it is only momentary. The aftermath inevitably sees the pain come back after just a few short weeks, days, or hours – and becomes more intense when it does return. Strategies under short-term focus include smoking and alcohol consumption.

- **Masking Emotions** – People who are afraid of being branded as weak or crazy often mask their true emotions as part of coping with stress. Similar to avoidance, these people bury their real feelings deep within, in a place within themselves where no other person can see or determine their pain. They put up happy smiles whenever they want to cry or break down. Masking emotions prevent a person from being fully understood by the people around them, becoming emotionally invisible and burying themselves in more masked pain.

- **Guarded Behaviors** – This type of maladaptive mechanism lets a person rely on a certain person or behavior to keep themselves safe from their fears and anxieties. These people are often afraid of harmful consequences, leading them to search for things, people, or behaviors who can assure them safety. Their guards are always up, preventing them from taking any risks and living fulfilling lives.

As I mentioned previously, these maladaptive strategies do not ever resolve the root cause of the person's anxiety-provoking problems. When used often, these negative coping strategies put further strain and stress on the person, negatively affecting them in every possible way. It has erroneous impacts on both their immediate surroundings, and more damagingly, their long-term outlook on life.

Dealing with Maladaptive Coping Mechanisms through Cognitive Behavioral Therapy

People inflicted with mental disturbances of any kind often utilize maladaptive coping mechanisms to deal with extreme stress and anxiety. But these non-coping mechanisms must ideally be changed into adaptive ones for the clients to cope with stress in a positive way.

But the problem lies in the client's inherent resistance to change, because of his or her reluctance to leave the artificial comforts afforded to them by the maladaptive coping mechanisms they are currently employing.

Cognitive behavioral therapy can be utilized to help a client recognize their maladaptive coping strategies and gradually turn them into adaptive coping. It is widely used as a tool in dealing with maladaptive thinking and coping.

The following phases under a CBT structured plan will help in getting therapists started in dealing with maladaptive coping mechanisms:

Monitoring One's Thoughts – The therapist may ask their client to check on his or her thoughts in response to anxiety-provoking situations. They could tell the client to keep track of the maladaptive coping ways they have been using to deal with their stress, fears, and anxiety.

Thought-Challenging – This is also known as cognitive restructuring. The therapist then guides a client in identifying maladaptive coping mechanisms, with reference to their own monitoring of thoughts. Once identified, the therapist asks the client to restructure or challenge these maladaptive thoughts by:

1. Looking at the pros and cons of worrying about a certain situation.

2. Evaluating any evidence which supports the client's maladaptive coping behaviors.

The client could be given some homework related to restructuring their own thoughts as well. These assignments could include keeping a record of how they used maladaptive coping in a particular situation.

Later on during the CBT session, both the client and therapist work together to understand reasons behind the client's maladaptive coping, challenging these thoughts to identify if they are appropriate or not.

Thought Replacement – After the client has fully grasped the realities of their negative thoughts and maladaptive coping, the therapist then gradually assists him or her in replacing them with positive coping strategies. The client might take some time to get used to the newer more positive thoughts, but it is well worth sticking to the process as the payoff will be highly desirable.

Evaluation – The therapist then evaluates how the client is making progress in using these new adaptive coping strategies. They may continue to provide small assignments to the client, or ask them to talk about the instances in which they finally learned to replace the maladaptive practices with more positive ones.

After successful CBT sessions, the client must be able to use healthier ways of dealing with stressful situations they encounter in daily life. They must be able to identify when they begin to cross over to the maladaptive side, and find ways to come back to positive coping strategies they now know.

Other Ways to Deal with Maladaptive Coping Mechanisms

Apart from CBT, here are some alternative ways a person may use to help themselves manage his or her maladaptive coping mechanisms on their own:

Thought Stopping – This is where a person comes up with a responsive action to stop maladaptive thoughts and non-coping from settling in. While experiencing a stressful situation, they can use a positive physical reaction or more productive thoughts to immediately halt the maladaptive behaviors from coming out.

For instance, they may tell themselves "Stop!" whenever they think of using aggression as a way to deal with the anxious situations they face. This triggers the person to halt the maladaptive thinking and stop it's subsequent behaviors from forming.

Distraction – When confronted by anxiety-provoking situations, the stressed-out person chooses to shift their focus onto safer activities, rather than engaging their thoughts and actions to maladaptive patterns. He or she can distract themselves away from maladaptive coping by doing activities such as writing, crafting, drawing, listening to music, for example. Activities which both distract the mind and are therapeutic towards a positive end.

Meditation – Guided contemplative meditation is a great way to help a person relax and enter a more positive state of mind. Not only does it stop triggering maladaptive behaviors, but it also improves the person's mood and helps the person focus on positive behaviors instead.

Using these three methods can greatly help a person in managing their own stressful situations and guides them into positive coping strategies on their own. These methods promote client independence towards realizing his or her own positive coping strategies, greatly improving the chance of staving off the negative thought patterns which once plagued them well into the future.

PART 2

ADVANCED COGNITIVE BEHAVIORAL THERAPY TECHNIQUES FOR PRACTICAL IMPLEMENTATION

By now, you should hopefully have a good grasp of what cognitive behavioral therapy is in a general sense. The following part to this book will now focus on the different techniques and approaches to CBT, as well as complimentary methods, which can be used to help a variety of people suffering from different types of mental health disturbances such as depression, anxiety, and stress.

CHAPTER 5

MULTIMODAL MODEL

Humans are naturally multifaceted beings. As such, problems which arise in our lives often tend to be complex and multifaceted in nature as well. With this in mind, therapies designed to help people deal with their complex problems must address not just one element of a person's being. It must look into several facets of his or her personality as well.

Multimodal therapy is among the CBT approaches wherein a person is taken care of holistically. It's an effective treatment which uses the totality of human personality to treat a person inflicted with mental disturbances. In this chapter, the basics of multimodal therapy and its practical implications will be discussed.

What is Multimodal Therapy?

Multimodal therapy is a treatment plan aimed at changing a person's behavior through incorporating several interrelated elements or "modalities" of one's personality.

Dr. Arnold Lazarus is a brilliant psychologist who came up with this comprehensive treatment plan. He also coined the term "behavior therapy", referring to his Multimodal Therapy as a treatment plan aimed at influencing the behaviors of a client.

Dr. Lazarus noted that many clients treated using traditional cognitive behavioral therapy have relapsed at some point in time. He then concluded that the psychotherapy treatments were missing certain areas, leaving vulnerable points in the client's personality which can sometimes lead to relapses after treatment had ended. Because of this, Dr. Lazarus came up with a more comprehensive approach to CBT that he called Multimodal Therapy.

Basic Principles of Multimodal Therapy – The Multimodal Model

Dr. Lazarus believed that humans are multifaceted and complex biological beings. Humans have several senses that enable us to appreciate the world around us. We know how to think, act, and relate with other human beings. We also experience a wide spectrum of emotions, ranging from positive to negative ones.

From these beliefs sprung an idea to classify certain elements of human beings which can be addressed to decipher negative thoughts and alter the behaviors of people suffering from mental disturbances. These elements are called modalities, and are listed as an acronym BASIC ID:

- **Behavior** – How a person acts towards life situations.

- **Affect** – The emotions a person is capable of showing.

- **Sensation** – How a person senses and appreciates the world. This consists of the five basic senses: smell, sight, touch, hearing, and taste.

- **Imagery** – Refers to a person's self-image, how they sees themselves, and their photographic thinking.

- **Cognition** – How a person thinks in terms of beliefs, attitudes, and words.

- **Interpersonal** – Describes how they relate to other people.

- **Drugs and Biology** – Portrays the general health and well-being of a person. Included in this modality are a person's diet, exercise, rest and sleep, and any medications taken.

These seven interrelated modalities form the Multimodal Model, which also forms the backbone of Multimodal Therapy.

Clients undergoing multimodal therapy are assessed holistically, based on the seven modalities. This ensures the therapy isn't just restricted to one or two personality dimensions, such as cognition and behavior only. Multimodal therapy is holistic in that it includes all necessary modalities which can affect how a person thinks and behaves as a whole.

By assessing and treating a person holistically, therapists have a higher chance of getting clients who are fully healed from their disruptive mental states to stay that way. Chances of relapse are low because the therapy is designed to cover every piece of the personality puzzle so to speak. To never miss important points in the client's multifaceted makeup.

How Multimodal Therapy Sessions Work

The therapy starts with the therapist's initial assessment of the client. Upon establishing rapport and getting to know the client broadly, the therapist proceeds to determining what the client's specific problems are.

The Multimodal Life History Inventory, a comprehensive assessment tool used to check the client's personality using the BASIC ID model as a guide, is given to the client. This 15-page assessment tool consists of the following sections:

- **General Information** – Includes questions about personal information.

- **Personal and Social History** – Family history, mental health history on both parental sides, relationships with parents and siblings, growing-up environment.

- **Description of Presenting Problem** – Questions about the client's main problem, what he or she is trying to solve, when the issue started and how severe it may be.

- **Expectations Regarding Therapy** – What the client wants to gain from the therapy, traits they would like to see in their therapist, how they view this therapy session in general.

- **Modality Analysis of Current Problems** – Includes sections for thoroughly evaluating the client based on the BASIC ID multimodal model. Direct questions, checklists, scales, and fill-in the blank questions form this part.

- **Description of Significant Memories and Experiences** – Any memories or related experiences which the client feels they need to share with the therapist, with respect to the problem at hand.

The second meeting starts with the therapist and client looking over the completed Multimodal Life History assessment tool. The therapist assists the client in completing any areas of the tool left blank. Together, they discuss the contents and the client's answers to the tool's questions. From there, the therapist gets a broader picture of the real problems engulfing the client's distressed mind.

A treatment plan is then mapped out for the client. The therapist bases these plans on the client's unique characteristics and personality based on the seven modalities. From there, they will look at the modalities in which they must focus on intensively, and shares these plans with the client.

At the start of each session, client and therapist review facts and insights learned from the last session. The client's progress is also evaluated. Then, client and therapist start addressing individual needs. The therapist may provide activities geared towards improving the client's outlook based on the difficulties he or she is experiencing in any of the seven modalities. The client may be given activities depending on their particular needs, such as talking, writing down thoughts, relaxation techniques, proper diet, and meditation.

Towards the end of each session, client and therapist both review what has been learned and what actions need to be taken for the next session. The therapist tapes each session, with the client's consent, in order to study the person's behavior further. They will also provide a copy of this tape to the client so they can review the session again at a later date.

One session of multimodal therapy lasts for a few hours typically, depending on the client's individual needs and progress. Timelines for the entire therapy program also varies from person to person, but typically lasts around 20-30 sessions on average.

Benefits of Multimodal Model Therapy

In my experience dealing with many forms cognitive self-improvement and therapeutic practices over the years, I have always found the more holistic approaches work the best. In this sense a Mutlimodal type strategy is one of my preferred choices when advising people who come to me with negative mental disturbances.

Multimodal therapy greatly benefits people suffering from mild to moderate cases of depression, anxiety, and substance abuse. This psychotherapy treatment works well when the affected person is willing to work together with his or her health care providers and therapists to come up with solutions to their multifaceted problems.

Here are some of the main advantages to using this psychotherapy method:

- Comprehensive and holistic approach to treating anxiety-laden clients.

- Lesser chances of relapse than classic CBT therapies.

- Flexible and highly individualized to suit each person's needs.

- Encourages active participation on the client's part.

If you are suffering from mild yet varied forms of mental disturbances and stress within your life, I would greatly advise you to seek out a professional to give this method a go. As I mentioned previously, it is one of my favorite approaches as it deals with a range of personality traits to help a person get over their issues in the most complete and natural way possible.

CHAPTER 6

REPROCESSING AND EMDR

Various life experiences form a human being's personality and helps shape his or her general outlook as a result. It is but normal to experience harsh realities in life. But when a person is faced with a traumatic experience, it could be so devastating that it robs them of their interest to continue experiencing life.

Adequate therapeutic help must be given to people suffering from traumatic life events in order to get their mental state back in better shape. EMDR is one effective treatment used in such cases, typically in conjunction with classic CBT sessions. This chapter provides an overview of EMDR and how it is used to treat clients.

What Is EMDR?

EMDR stands for Eye Movement Desensitization and Reprocessing. This therapeutic approach is chiefly used and originally designed for clients with post-traumatic stress disorders.

EMDR is a set of protocols which combine rhythmic bilateral eye movements and tactile stimulation to activate the brain, reconnect the neurophysiological system, and relieve the person of their traumatic experiences.

American psychologist Francine Shapiro first developed EMDR in 1987. She noticed that side to side movements of her eyes appeared to slowly relieve her of negative emotions related to her own unpleasant experiences and memories.

After conducting several experiments and research, she validated that her discovery was promising with regards to the general public. She began developing standardized procedures and reported success with a number of trauma victims who had benefited from her EMDR sessions in 1989. Today, research regarding EMDR methods continue in an effort to cement and establish this treatment.

Basic Principles of EMDR – REM and Thought Reprocessing

When a person suffers from severe stress and trauma, their brain's information processing system becomes imbalanced. This renders him or her to experience distressing psychological symptoms which disrupt the normal thought processes. This further leads to the person having difficulty processing what has happened to them.

Inadequate processing of stressful events creates negative emotions which can become trapped and suppressed in a person's subconscious mind. Memories of these events become a trigger for the person to repeatedly experience pain, as if the event occurred freshly again.

I write about this concept in greater detail in other books, but the brain has very little ability to distinguish events in an emotional sense with regards to the human perception of time. The primal regions of brains limbic system, especially the amygdala will fire up its activity and start the cascade of chemical/hormone release and subsequent emotional response in exactly the same way, regardless of whether the person is experiencing the event in the present moment, during a past memory, or even a perceived point in the future.

EMDR is based on Rapid Eye Movement (REM), a natural phenomenon which occurs to the human mind during sleep. Sleeping humans unconsciously experience rapid eye movements which aids in dream creation and subsequently helps in processing painful events, bringing relief to ordinary stress-inducing conditions.

But people suffering from extreme trauma and emotional stress are largely unable to utilize REM during sleep to process their thoughts. This leads to a disruption in relieving these stressful conditions.

Dr. Shapiro discovered that rhythmic eye movements mimic REM and trigger a desensitizing effect on a person thinking about extremely stressful life events. This, combined with other stimulation techniques, gently help a traumatized person's brain in reprocessing its thoughts on the particular cause of trauma.

How EMDR Therapy Sessions Work

EMDR works to slowly release suppressed stressful situations residing on a person's nervous system. After unlocking negative memories, it aids the brain in properly reprocessing these experiences. Thought processes are slowly "reprocessed" by means of eye stimulation, bilateral movements, and tactile sound stimulation.

The EMDR therapist will initially ask the client to recall traumatic events that linger and haunt their mind. They then gently guide the client in recounting the negative feelings, thoughts, and memories related to that event. By doing so, they are already guiding the client in releasing the suppressed negative energy brought about by extremely traumatic situation they have experienced.

After this initial stage, the therapist will proceed to the thought reprocessing exercises. They will take hold of the client's fingers and holds them a few inches from the person's face and in front of their field of vision. They will then wave the fingers repeatedly in a left-and-right motion and instruct the client to follow this movement with their eyes. The therapist may also make use of hand tapping movements or musical stimulation at this point.

As the client follows the back-and-forth finger motions, they will begin to focus more closely on the stressful situation and start to gently reprocess it in their mind. The therapist also simultaneously and gradually guides the person in replacing their thoughts with more pleasant ones.

The client ideally must be at peace with his or her feelings regarding this stressful life event after the session is over. Their painfully suppressed emotions should start to gradually shift to a more optimistic one over the course of the therapy.

Sessions usually last for 50-90 minutes once or twice weekly. This process can go on for around 1-3 months, depending on the severity of each client's mental disturbance.

Benefits of Reprocessing and EMDR

EMDR usually proves to be most beneficial for clients suffering from Post-Traumatic Stress Disorder (PTSD), mild to severe anxiety or panic attacks, phobias, eating disorders, and substance intoxication. Advantages of using EMDR therapy include:

- Heals the mind from overloaded negative memories.

- Helps neutralize negative responses to unpleasant life memories.

- Aids in peaceful resolution of painful and negative mental conflicts.

- Provides fast and lasting relief from extremely stressful life situations.

EMDR combined with cognitive behavioral therapy will no doubt lead to a better mental function and healthier behavioral responses to previous negative experiences. As with all of the techniques I have detailed within this book, implementing them as a standalone treatment will certainly aid in relieving much mental anguish. However combining a number of these strategies in a way which fits a person best, will always garner the greatest results in the long run.

CHAPTER 7

RATIONAL THERAPY METHOD

"People and things do not upset us, rather we upset ourselves by believing that they can upset us"

(Albert Ellis)

As we have already seen, an individual's emotions are greatly affected by their thoughts. What the mind perceives about a situation translates to feelings which, in turn, fuel a person's behavior. So when a mentally disturbed person thinks about a stressful situation, their mind becomes crowded with unpleasant thoughts which eventually gives way to negative feelings and behaviors.

Rational Therapy Method, also known as Rational Emotive Behavior Therapy (REBT), can help correct these cognitive and emotional disturbances. This chapter presents the facts regarding REBT and how it can help in transforming a person's behavior and emotions.

What Is Rational Emotive Behavioral Therapy?

Rational Emotive Behavioral Therapy is a treatment plan which harnesses the cognitive mind's power to reshape a person's core beliefs. This, in turn, also reshapes the person's emotions and behaviors. REBT actually laid the foundation for cognitive behavioral therapy concepts.

REBT was introduced by American psychologist Albert Ellis in 1955. His theory about rational emotive behavior was met with surprise, for during this time, the role of cognition in developing emotions was yet unknown to the world of psychology.

Within this therapy, mentally disturbed clients are believed to exhibit irrational cognitive beliefs which lead them to all sorts of negative emotions. By changing these core beliefs into more rational ones, mentally disturbed clients now have a chance to view their problems realistically, ultimately leading them to better emotions and behaviors.

Basic Principles of REBT – The Cognition-Emotion Link

It's all in a person's mind – how he or she thinks about a particular situation brings forth the related emotions, and shapes their attitudes towards that situation. This is the main premise upon which Dr. Ellis built his Rational Emotive Behavioral theory.

REBT presupposes that negative situations alone do not cause negative behaviors in a person. But rather it is how these situations are perceived which brings about negative behaviors. Impaired cognition brings about emotional disturbance, which leads to disruptive behavior patterns.

Core beliefs spring from a person's cognitive efforts to understand the events happening around them. These beliefs are often developed early on in life and are influenced by various events a person has experienced. As time passes, beliefs which were formed are reinforced and continue to subconsciously affect the person's behaviors and perceptions into adulthood.

REBT helps bring a person's subconscious, irrational beliefs into their conscious awareness. In doing so, these three guiding principles known as the ABCs of REBT are used:

1. **Adverse Event/Activating Event** – The event/s which initially triggered the person's emotional disturbances.

2. **Beliefs** – These are the core beliefs attached to the person's activating events. Often, these consists of irrational beliefs such as:

    - Self-condemnation – "I am a stupid person."

    - Low tolerance to frustrating situations – "I can't handle this/I can't do it."

    - Irrational demands for comfort, love, success, and approval – "I SHOULD have this."

3. **Consequences** – Activating events and their corresponding irrational beliefs give rise to negative consequences such as anxiety, stress, low self-esteem, and depression.

The ABCs of REBT are used as a guide to dispel negative behaviors. Unpleasant and painful emotions are reversed by helping the person develop positive thoughts and behaviors.

How REBT Therapy Sessions Work

REBT's goal is to help a person gain rational insights about past events which have negatively shaped their emotions and behaviors. Rational therapy sessions undertake three basic steps very similar to the general cognitive behavioral therapy systems:

1) Identifying Irrational Beliefs

The client's personal negative thoughts and beliefs are slowly uncovered by the therapist. The client is asked to recall unpleasant events which led to his or her feelings of depression or anxiety. They will then verbalize their problems and articulate how they think about them in the clearest manner possible.

2) Challenging Mistaken Beliefs Through Disputation

Once the underlying root causes and beliefs have been identified, a therapist then proceeds to help the client think deeper about them. The therapist uses a process known as disputation, wherein they will ask straightforward questions to the client. They will then guide the client in recognizing other ways to think about these problems in order to dispel the negative thoughts currently associated with them.

This part of the therapeutic process may take a longer period of time, depending on the client's responses. It could also seem a bit daunting, as the person is required to face their own disruptive thought patterns and try to change their thinking to a more realistic one. The therapist should guide them all the way until the person begins to gains proper insight about their own thought patterns and corresponding behavioral changes.

3) **Recognizing Negative Thought Patterns and Changing Them to More Realistic Ones**

After a series of sessions, the client must be able to start seeing their negative thought patterns in a new light. They realize that the mistakes of the past cannot be undone. Their thinking shifts to accepting what has happened, knowing that mistakes are an inevitable parts of life. Also that learning from these mistakes instead of dwelling on them is the only real road to peace of mind. They will finally learn healthier ways to think about unpleasant events which will also inevitably happen in the future.

Rational therapy method sessions usually take 40 to 60 minutes once or twice per week. Length of therapy depends on each individual person, usually taking a few months for a mentally disturbed person to be fully healed.

Benefits of Rational Therapy Method

Rational emotive behavioral therapy is best suited for clients undergoing depression, social anxiety, low self-esteem and substance abuse. Below are the advantages of this therapy method:

- Goal-oriented therapy designed to change a person's outlook towards their life.

- Helpful for clients willing to actively work with his therapy provider.

- Brings lasting changes to the mentally disturbed person.

- Low incidences of relapse after successful treatment completion.

CHAPTER 8

DIALECTICAL THERAPY

Human emotion is unquestionably a very powerful thing. We cannot escape the effect our limbic legacy has over us. The structures within the "old mammalian brain" such as the amygdala, still have very primal influences over us today. From the feelings of love, cooperation and compassion, to fear, anxiety and anger.

Intense emotions are natural, and experienced by all people throughout our lives. It could be happier feelings, such as when a long lost relative finally returns home or when a new born baby is brought into the world. The flip side of this are the sadder times, such as when a loved one passes away or when a person experiences traumatic life events.

Emotions are so powerful that they sometimes lead people to doing things they didn't expect to do. Such things may include suicidal tendencies, as the strong depression a person can feel inclines them to consider taking their own life.

Dialectical Therapy, also known as DBT or Dialectical Behavior Therapy, is one psychological approach used to treat clients with inclinations such as these. This final chapter of this book presents what DBT is, and how it is designed to help suicidal people heal.

What is Dialectical Therapy?

Dialectical Behavioral Therapy (DBT) is a form of talk therapy used as a gold standard in treating clients with Borderline Personality Disorder. It was developed by Marsha M. Linehan in the late 1980s.

DBT is a cognitive-behavioral treatment plan aimed at helping a person manage difficult and swinging emotions. This is done through activities which encourage identification, balance, acceptance, and change in emotional and behavioral life aspects.

Basic Principles of Dialectical Therapy - Balancing, Accepting, and Changing Emotions

Dialectical therapy works to improve a client's emotions and combat the desire to jump into sudden harmful behaviors arising from conflicting thought processes.

Clients with Borderline Personality Disorder (BPD) often benefit from dialectical behavioral therapy. One hallmark symptom of BPD is emotion so intense that it causes the person to act in harmful and destructive ways. If this behavior type persists, it eventually leads to failed relationships, self-injury, bursts of anger, and suicidal inclinations.

The following is a list of the main principles surrounding dialectical therapy in helping people overcome these extremely intense emotions:

- **Using Dialectics to Balance Out Conflicting Emotions**

Dialectical therapy uses dialectics in managing people's extremely volatile emotions. Dialectics is an approach which attempts to balance opposite emotional positions and decipher how conflicting emotions can go together.

An example of dialectics use is when therapists accept their clients for who they are without any judgment. At the same time, they also recognize that changes must be implemented in order to bring their clients back to a better state of mind and health. By creating a balance between acceptance and change, they're able to more objectively heal their client's mentally disturbed minds.

DBT therapists strive to let their clients recognize these dialectic tendencies and apply them to their conflicting emotions after they've primarily identified them.

- **Accepting and Understanding Oneself**

Most people do not truly understand why mentally-disturbed individuals behave in the ways they do, especially when this is in a self-destructive manner (as in the case of suicidal people).

Mentally-disturbed individuals often know their behaviors are viewed differently by the majority of people. In spite of that, they seek much-needed acceptance and understanding from the people around them. At times, they themselves cannot even accept what they're doing.

Dialectical therapy focuses on helping the person gain self-acceptance and understanding. Therapists do so by explaining that the mentally-disturbed person's behaviors are actually sensible. Behaviors were learned as their own ways of dealing with extremely traumatic events in their lives, making them sensible enough to be accepted and understood by others. But that is not to say they are productive and beneficial.

- **Changing the Person's Emotions and Behaviors**

Once the person has learned to accept himself or herself and be accepted by others, the change process starts. Harmful behaviors are slowly replaced by safer ones through various change techniques. Thought challenging is a common practice used to help clients move from their unpleasant emotions towards better, more productive ones.

Dialectical therapy is one of the most compassionate types of psychotherapy which lets the person know and feel they are understood. This subsequently leads to a behavioral and emotional shift for the better.

How Dialectical Therapy Sessions Work

Dialectical behavioral therapy works in a very similar manner to cognitive behavioral therapy. Both methods attempt to let the client recognize their emotions and think in a more realistic manner in order to change their behaviors.

Each dialectical behavioral therapy treatment plan often teaches clients these two important things:

1.   Life skills which are important to moving towards life goals.

2.   The means and ability to integrate these skills into daily life.

Clients will typically go through four main components of DBT when undertaking this form of therapy, which are as follows:

Individual DBT therapy – This is where the client is asked to focus on his or her emotions, encouraging them to talk and release any pent-up and mixed-up feelings and emotions. Therapists help the client get motivation to continue pursuing the therapy for their own good. Individual sessions are one-to-one talks which usually last for 60-90 minutes.

Skills training groups – The client also participates in a class-like therapy setting which assists them in learning more functional behavioral skills. The therapists teach these skills and assign various homework for the clients to experience using them in real life. Clients attend sessions either once or twice a week for at least 2-3 hours each time.

Skills taught to clients include regulating emotions, interpersonal effectiveness, pain tolerance in intense situations, and becoming fully aware of the present moment. Therapists may incorporate other skills as they see fit.

DBT phone sessions – Clients are allowed to call their therapists for special coaching whenever they feel the need to get some further guidance. Therapist's lines are always open for techniques, tips, and ways to properly use the skills their clients have learned during individual and group therapy sessions.

Consultation for therapists – This is actually a component not participated in by the clients. Rather, this is a meeting for therapists to support each other. Dealing with numerous mentally-disturbed clients can be truly overwhelming and testing at times. This is why therapists need to meet on a weekly basis to make sure that they are still able to give the best possible care for their clients.

Clients with DBT treatments often have several problems at hand. So, therapists prioritize DBT treatments in order to fully cover every problem they're experiencing. Prioritization happens in the following order:

1) **Behaviors leading to self-destruction or harm** – suicidal tendencies.

2) **Behaviors preventing the client from receiving proper treatment** – arriving late to sessions, absenteeism, non-collaborative behaviors.

3) **Behaviors interfering with quality of life** – relationship concerns, household problems, financial outlooks.

4) **Replacement of old skills with newer, more effective ones** - standard CBT behavioral change exercises.

The duration of the entire dialectical behavioral treatment may last 3-4 months, depending on the client's mental health and behavioral progress. If the process is successful, the clients end up being able to control their emotions better, think more positively towards each life situation, and act more appropriately to the benefit themselves and of those around them.

Benefits of Dialectical Therapy Method

Dialectical behavioral therapy is regarded as the gold standard in caring for clients plagued with borderline personality disorders. It is also effective for clients dealing with other types of depression and mania. Advantages of using dialectical therapy method include:

- An effective way of overcoming intense behavioral symptoms.

- Provides self-awareness, validation, and tolerance - things depressed clients are often deprived of.

- A transparent therapy which can help clients feel safe and at ease.

- Low relapse cases after completion of treatment.

- Allows clients to become collaborative partners in caring for themselves.

Clients often return to their normal, undisturbed mindsets after completion of DBT therapy. Relapsing to emotional flare-ups and harmful behaviors are not usually seen as clients already know how to take care of the root situations which lead to these kinds of emotions.

That is not to say this method is easy, like every other treatment strategy outlined in this book. It will take careful and consistent work towards achieving the results so desirable to the clients. Especially with regards to Dialectical Therapy, as it aims to help some of the most vulnerable individuals in need of help today.

SUMMARY

So in summary of the techniques and topics discussed in this book, what actually is Cognitive Behavioral Therapy? As I described in the opening chapter, CBT is a combined psychotherapy and behavioral therapy treatment aimed at changing the way in which a person thinks and acts towards stressful situations they may find themselves in.

This approach differs from many other models of mental treatment, in the sense it is much more of a collaborative effort between the client and therapist. CBT is designed for the person to resolve their problems as naturally as possible by working through the mutually agreed upon behavioral exercises and thought processes.

It was Dr. Aaron T. Beck who originally discovered the effects of a CBT style therapy when working with depressed patients during the 1960's. What he actually discovered was the impact "Automatic Negative Thoughts" have over a persons sate, which was almost always the starting point of depressive and high anxiety thinking.

These people usually hold a combined negative outlook not only on themselves, but also their surroundings, as well as the prospects for the future. These tendencies are usually developed within childhood, during the sponge like adolescent years when we are attributing meaning (often incorrectly) to the events happening around us. If these instances aren't freshly appraised and re-evaluated later on in life, they can persist well into adult hood.

This is what CBT attempts to rectify, these negative thought patterns which may or may not have any real logical basis in reality. Well certainly not beneficial ones to the patient. Therapy will typically last no longer than a few months, with sessions of 30-60 minutes every couple of weeks being sufficient in making the necessary changes to thinking .

It's not just anxiety and depression which CBT aims to treat though. Since discovering this method within the 1960's, it has since proved useful in aiding people with all kinds of mental disturbances including, but not limited too: Phobias, Post-Traumatic Stress Disorder, Obsessive-Compulsive Disorder, Alcoholism, Insomnia, Anger Management.

That being said, patients are certainly categorized and treatments prioritized according to the most serious and high risk cases. This is of course people with acute forms of anxiety and depression.

In cases such as these, more advanced and complimentary CBT treatment methods are often implemented to aid recovery. These strategies include Multimodel Therapy, which incorporates a multifaceted personality approach in dealing with mental health issue. EMDR, which uses Eye Movement Desensitization and Reprocessing in order to help clients with post-traumatic stress disorders. Rational Emotive Behavioral Therapy, which helps to reshape a person's core beliefs. And Dialectical Behavioral Therapy, which was developed to help those most at risk from suicidal tendencies.

It is up to the therapist to decide what the best course of action is with regards to each individual case. A person may require a single method of treatment, or a combination of the various CBT style techniques. But as always, a holistic and natural approach seems to be the most beneficial and successful path to full recovery.

CONCLUSION

"The greatest discovery of my generation, is that a human being
can alter life, by altering his attitudes of mind"

(William James)

I certainly do not want to trivialize the seriousness of human
cognitive distress and disturbance with random self-help quotes.
But this William James passage I find fitting. Unlike the other
psychological topics I have previously written on, cognitive
behavioral therapy has a much more important role to play.

That being said, I do still believe a person's happiness, and ultimately
peace of mind, is predicated almost entirely by how they think. It's
perception which counts the most. External events are just that.
External, neutral, meaningless. Until we give them one.

The problem stems from exactly where we may have picked up
this conditioning. It's all too often adverse childhood experiences
or simply bad programming from teachers and parents or society
in general. So rectifying and rewiring these cognitive mishaps is
paramount.

Again, I'm not suggesting this is an easy process to undergo, no
positive psychology journey ever is. But as I always point out, it
will be well worth the effort setting out down this road to begin

with. Gaining harmony in your life is the ultimate payoff. From a position of calmness, contentment and joy, everything is possible. Or at least manageable.

I share the opinion of many others, that CBT techniques are some of the best methods available for ensuring people who suffer from persistent and significant negative thinking, get to a better place. Hopefully you now have a clearer idea of what some of these practices entail, and how to implement the simpler ones yourself.

However it goes without saying, that any serious and severe downturn in a person's mental state should ALWAYS be dealt with by the proper health care professionals. You should always seek consultancy from your doctor if you believe you are possibly getting to this stage. There is never a good reason to suffer alone.

Whatever path you decide to take, I wish you the very best of luck.

BONUS CHAPTERS

(From 'Emotional Intelligence: A Psychologist's Guide')

CHAPTER 4

TAKING INVENTORY OF YOUR EMOTIONAL STATE

"Educating the mind without educating the heart is no education at all"

(Aristotle)

One of the most important things you can do when initially starting out on your emotional intelligence enhancing journey is to take stock of what you are currently feeling. There is no right or wrong answers here in terms of what come up. As our limbic legacy show us, humans are inherently emotional creatures and suppressing them is almost impossible to do entirely.

However you do have control over the way you react to these tendencies, the thoughts and behaviors after the fact. The following factors should help you take a closer look into how to identify and deal with these feelings when they do arise to ultimately move you to the next level in your E.Q. journey.

Acknowledge Your Emotions

The first thing to do when attempting to increase your personal E.Q. levels is to get good at acknowledging and perceiving the emotions that you are feeling. This is the starting point for every model and framework of E.Q.

Whenever I feel an emotion arise within me I always take a pause and acknowledge its presence, I take a moment and really feel it so I can understand and label it in my mind. This isn't the same as reacting or acting upon the emotion just yet, but I want to know why it may have arisen and if it could be useful to me. If it's a feeling of anger, fear or frustration I do not deny or try to hide it, but instead acknowledge its presence and dismiss it as not being productive and move on.

If you start to dwell on emotions such as these you will quickly fall into a negative spiral thought process that will have you framing everything in a pessimistic light before you know it. I used to play out entire imaginary scenarios in my head of something going badly and the knock-on effects that I 'knew' it would have, only to realize that it NEVER worked out that badly and that I'd fabricated it all in my mind. Sound familiar?

If on the other hand it is an emotion of excitement, joy or anticipation, I also pause for a moment, acknowledge and label what it is that I'm feeling and try to cultivate and utilize it if I think it will benefit the situation such as situational empathy (which we will get onto later).

It is also important to take responsibility for these emotions that you are feeling either way, good or bad. Know that it is something inside of you which is eliciting such a response and that you have to deal with it and not sweep it under the carpet so to speak. This is usually the most challenging step for people, but it is also the most rewarding. Yes it maybe some outside influence or stimulus that sparked the response in the first place, but remember that the emotions you are feeling are coming from within you and that it's your responsibility to deal with them

Understand That You Are Not Your Emotions

So following on from that, you also need to constantly remind yourself that the emotions which arise within you and the conscious entity which interprets them are two very different things. Most people walk around in somewhat of a waking sleep for the most part completely at the mercy of any feeling, thought or emotion that pops into their head.

You have to understand that many thoughts and emotions will pass through you almost on a second by second basis, but again it's entirely your choice on how you perceive and choose to react to them.

There is also a very large egoic element to this process as well. Thoughts and feelings of jealously for another person or fear of performing a task is really just your ego trying to keep your preconceived notions about the world intact and keep you operating within your comfort zone. This is a topic for much greater discussion i.e. regarding the tactics to counteract such self-sabotaging behavior, but needless to say that detaching yourself from your overall emotional state is very a beneficial thing to do.

Learn to Forgive Yourself & Others

"Life becomes easier when you learn to accept an apology you never got"

(Robert Brault)

Again, along the same lines as letting go of a negative emotion that arises within you, people have a great tendency to hold onto what they perceive to be negative acts that they have either committed themselves or others against them. Holding onto this ill feeling again serves absolutely no purpose to you in the immediate future and certainly not the long run. *"Holding onto anger is like drinking poison and expecting the other person to die"* as the Buddha so aptly put it.

If there was one thing that got me ahead in my business life so quickly it was this concept. Once I stopped getting caught up with what I thought I deserved from a situation or others around me and started pushing ahead regardless, I made so much more

COGNITIVE BEHAVIORAL THERAPY

progress. You can't stop and throw stones at every dog that barks, and that includes yourself when you mess up.

This isn't just applicable to adult and business life either, it's relates to everyone young or old. If I had taken heed of this advice when I was growing up I know I would have had better overall relationships with school/college friends and family alike. That's not to say things were necessarily that bad, but they could have been better, or at least I could have saved myself a great deal of heart ache and stress along the way.

Don't Get Involved in Negative Self-Talk

As I mentioned above, letting negative self talk get out of hand is a very bad habit to take up. I would say that it is the one thing that plagues humanity more than anything. We often talk ourselves out of things before we've had a chance to start them. Again this comes down to letting negative thoughts and emotions cloud our thinking to a point of almost no escape. You have to stop this in its tracks as quickly as possible if you want to build high overall levels of emotional intelligence.

This also includes negative self-talk and 'gossip' regarding other people. In danger of sounding like one of your parents or school teachers here, you don't need me to tell you this is a worthless exercise and one that will ultimately bring your E.Q. level down with it. No one is perfect; just make a point of catching yourself when you start to talk in this way.

Also along the same lines as the above, you must try and do your best not to judge others where ever possible. This actually freed me greatly in a psychological sense when I managed to stop doing it a few years ago. I never thought of myself as an overly judgmental person but I still realized I would do it from time to time. But stopping myself altogether from judging anyone I came across in even the smallest way saves me so much mental energy and almost certain daily miss judgment.

Nowadays I simply let others go about their day in their own way without even the slightest judging thought about their behavior. That is not to say that I tolerate bad behavior or that I do not try and empathize with people and attempt to understand their situation better, which is critical to building fruitful relationships. But I don't judge them with regards to how they got to where they are, I never walked in their shoes or went through the struggles they did so I let them do the talking on this one.

Again this isn't some "holier than thou" situation, I'm not perfect and do very occasionally catch myself automatically judging someone. I just now catch it very early and stop myself in my tracks straight away. It's so much more liberating when you do.

BONUS CHAPTER

(From 'NLP: A Psychologist's Guide')

CHAPTER 7

LOOP BREAKS & PATTERN INTERRUPTS

The brain is undoubtedly an extremely complex organ within the human body. It is required to perform an incredible number of calculations every second even during mundane tasks like guiding the various parts of the body for movement in simple motor skills all the way to making crucial and complex decisions in real time. The brain undertakes millions of these interconnected decisions every single day thereby making it one of the most powerful pieces of biological machinery we have.

However we still do not fully understand the extent of it's complexity and inner workings. One thing we do know is that the brain is solely responsible for enabling people to develop thought patterns and habits that ultimately dictate not only their daily behaviors but also their thinking patterns. It does this in an attempt to optimize a person's day-to-day movements and thought processes, but these short cuts aren't always beneficial.

In order to form these "loops" or "patterns" the brain undertakes several processes that help it both develop a certain habit and make it a part of routine life. In this segment, we will start by taking a brief look at the meaning of cognition in general, which is fairly critical when it comes to NLP. Cognition is simply the study of how the brain perceives information and represents it within the persons mind. It tells us how the brain functions and helps in putting that information to use.

The branch of study that deals with establishing a relationship between learning and cognition is known as neuropsychology, an area of study I once specialized in myself. Neurology has intrigued scientists for as long as the concept has been around with many psychologists having studied its intricacies for decades now. Right from classical conditioning described by Pavlov and John Watson to the operant conditioning of B F Skinner, each one presented theories that described how the human brain works and learns.

It is no secret that a person's daily habits and thinking routines will ultimately dictate how productive and successful they are. However habits are impartial, they will either help a person attain their desired results and remain persistent in pursuing them. Or they will ensure they continue getting the average/poor results they have always gotten. As Dr Bandler pointed out "Brains aren't designed to get results; they just go in directions".

In terms of general behavior it is usually just a case of learning your ABC's so to speak i.e. learning the sequence of the Antecedent, Behavior and Consequence. This concept was originally based on Skinner's model of cognition, antecedent, behavior and consequence being the three main steps involved in developing a habit. In a nutshell they are described as follows:

Antecedents

Antecedents are stimuli that precede a behavior or reaction. They are situations and circumstances that cause a person to behave in a certain manner. Antecedents determine the outcome of a certain behavior by inducing it automatically.

In simpler terms, antecedents are people and situations that solicit a certain reaction or behavior. They are what lay down the basis for habits, they hold the key to how a person reacts to any given situation.

Antecedents are studied to know whether the reaction is a result of positive reinforcement or punishment by and large. Having this knowledge makes it easier to predict future behavior. It is fairly simple to manipulate antecedents in order to evoke the desired behavior.

Behavior

The second component within the habit development model is behavior. Behavior is the response provided to the stimulus. It is meant to serve two main purposes namely to get something that a person desires or to avoid getting something they do not.

It is important to note that almost all behavior is learned from significant others. Some is reactionary but all is observable and measurable.

This means that behavior is both visible to others and is a reflection of the person's mind. For example, if a person is angry then their behavior will come through in the form of a changed facial expression or an angry physical reaction. This behavior differs from person to person and is not constant, but rather based on their learned behavior through observing others during past experiences.

As I mention, behavior is also measurable. This means that it is possible for another person to describe the behavior after observation. For example, a person can observe another person getting angry and describe his reaction. This behavior can be altered to give away a desirable outcome.

Consequence

Consequence is the final component and is a result of the behavior phase. It can be viewed as the environment's reaction to a certain behavior. A consequence will be a direct result of the behavioral action. For example, if a person reacts to a certain situation in a negative manner then the consequence is bound to be negative. Say a person slams a vase on the floor out of anger then it is obvious that the vase will break and the person will have to clean it up. Consequence is also measurable just like behavior.

Basically if you are fully aware of the process I described above you can alter it for your own benefit. It involves understanding the cues, following a routine and availing the consequence/reward. The key here is to aim for the desired results but change the antecedent and rewards, then the behavior will automatically change accordingly.

For example, if you are trying to learn a new skill, but buying books in order to achieve this is not inspiring you enough to study the material then changing over to online classes may inspire you to better effect.

Similarly, you can also change the reward in order to modify the behavior. For example, when trying to excel in a competitive exam, you can look forward to treating yourself to a toy/clothes you have wanted to buy for a long time. Both can work as a motivating factor for you to modify the behavior enough.

The above method works great for changing more general behavioral patterns I find. However we are more concerned with the thinking habits here as opposed to just the behavioral, although they somewhat go hand in hand. That is what real NLP seeks to accomplish. For that you need to view things in a slightly different way, to adopt another approach.

TOTE Process

With regards to the thinking process in NLP there is a similar structure that the mind follows. It's sometimes described as the path of least resistance approach and is made up of four components the Trigger, Operation, Test and Exit. I'll elaborate on each in a little more detail below:

Trigger

Similar to the ABC sequence of behavior learning I described above, the TOTE process starts with an antecedent or cue known here as the trigger. In NLP it's also called the 'Anchor' from time to time and once again relates to the impetus or stimulus which starts off the pattern.

Operation

The operation once again like the ABC process, relates to the behavior portion of the pattern and the thinking habit that we undertake.

Test

However this time the mind performs a 'test' of that preceding behavior to identify whether the intended outcome was met or not. Did the person get the desired result from that action? If the answer is 'no', then the person will continue through with the behavior cycle until they do.

Exit

If the answer was 'yes' to the test stage, then a person will simply move on with their behavior and proceed to close this thinking pattern loop so to speak. This completion stage must happen in order to not continually go round in circles.

This is how we typically form habits in thinking which can be very powerful cycles especially if built and reinforced over a long period of time. It isn't necessarily a bad thing if this thinking loop is genuinely a beneficial one, but if it is not then it can be quite destructive. We can see this quite clearly in individuals with high obsessive compulsive tendencies (OCD).

In any case these cycles can be reasonably difficult to break but it's imperative that you do so in order to move on from a negative cycle. That is one of the main tenants of NLP, breaking these negative thought patterns to replace with better and more beneficial ones. This process certainly played a critical role to my overall success. When I really learnt how to pattern interrupt.

Thought Pattern Interrupts

The idea here is to disrupt a negative thought pattern as early on in the cycle/sequence as possible, more specifically between the trigger and the operation. Regardless it must be completed before the testing phase of the condition, to say that you must disrupt it before the mind tries to test the original operation pattern otherwise any attempt to break the sequence will be of little use as the pattern is almost completed.

The pattern interrupts aren't that difficult to implement and it is simply about stopping your train of thought and thinking about something different, butting in on your own thought process/conversation you are having within your own head.

Like Richard Bandler suggests, we are simply trying to change the direction of the mind and reprogram it as we do. You are not removing the old pattern per se, but rather redirecting around it.

Go big!

The idea is to make this interrupt as big and bold as possible. If there is one mistake I see from people who try this method is that they are too weak with their disrupting action and it isn't enough to fully divert their thinking. Especially if it is a long term entrenched habit of thought they are trying to break.

Try a loud clap of the hands or loud cough. If the cycle which is trying to be broken is a negative thought process with depressive emotions attached to it, then try breaking the pattern with a little dance/jig or a laugh. Try to inject humor into the disrupt as it is completely counter to the original and unwanted behavior and congruent with the newer, happier thought process.

Timing is Everything

As I described above, timing is everything here. You need to ensure you catch the trigger phase as accurately as you can as it will be key to identifying when you need to employ the pattern disrupt. In essence this should be directly after and as soon as possible following on from when the trigger is spotted.

However in reality this is likely to be a very short period of time so you really have to be a keen observant throughout the day to catch them when they do occur. For me it was usually some thought or memory which popped into my head that would start the cycle, especially the negative ones.

If I let it continue, my emotions and physiology would start to change when in it would be too late. I have now learnt to catch this right before this transition takes place i.e right after the trigger thought/memory and replace my momentary operation/behavior to a more positive one.

Rinse & Repeat

However that is simply not enough in my experience, just catching the cycle once. The real payoff comes from repeating this cycle over and over until the new behavior pattern becomes habitual and you start to see the results you are looking for.

So make sure you perform whatever interrupt you have chosen until it becomes second nature to you, until you no longer have to think about it. You have to bring the skill into the "Unconscious Competence" phase when performing it. That is when the new direction of thought and subsequent behavior will really take hold.

This general approach was taken from hypnotherapists such as Milton Erickson who used pattern interrupts to disrupt the waking thinking patterns of their participants. They would lead a persons inner monologue down a familiar path before disrupting the line of questioning leaving the persons unconscious mind waiting for the logical next step of the pattern to occur, but it never comes. This can be a powerful enough confusion of the mind which puts a certain percentage of the population into a hypnotic trance.

You are not attempting to go that far with yourself and it's almost impossible to do it on your own, but the general thought pattern interrupt is designed to work along the same lines. But this time to disrupt a familiar negative thought pattern such as anger and replace with a more positive and beneficial one.

www.ingramcontent.com/pod-product-compliance
Lightning Source LLC
Chambersburg PA
CBHW062010280526
45787CB00005B/2055